ABSOLUTELY ENTERTAINING

ISBN 1-889491-04-7
Library of Congress Catalog Card Number: 96-70275

*Distributed to the trade in the United States, Canada,
and Mexico by:*
Book Nippan
1123 Dominguez Street, Unit K
Carson, CA 90746
Fax   310 604 1134

Published by:
Supon Design Editions
1700 K Street, NW, Suite 400
Washington, DC 20006
Tel   202 882 6540
Fax   202 882 6541

Printed in Hong Kong

absolutely
ENTERTAINING!

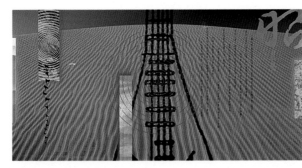

**THE WORLD OF
ENTERTAINMENT
GRAPHICS**

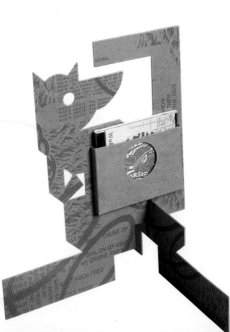

SUPON DESIGN GROUP

Project Director   Supon Phornirunlit
Communications Director   Wayne Kurie
Publications Director   Debbi Savitt
Art Director   Supon Phornirunlit
Jacket Designer   Alexander Chang
Book Designer   Alexander Chang
Editor   Greg Varner
Writer   Linda Klinger
Agent Representative   HK Marketing, Los Angeles, CA

Front Cover Contributors:

(Clockwise from top left)

Viva Italia!, Modern Dog, (Page 78)

Film Collections Logo, Sabin Design, (Page 31)

IBM's Olympic Sponsorship Identity, Supon Design Group, (Page 110)

"The Four Chinese Beauties" CD Packaging, Alan Chan Design Company, (Page 46)

"Working Without Annette" CD Packaging and P.O.P. Display Unit, Sayles Graphic Design, (Page 60)

Back Cover Contributors:

(Clockwise from top left)

"Candles" Video for "Phantom", Echo Advertising & Marketing Inc., (Page 86)

Kid's Presentation Brochure, Laurie Kellihar/World Egg, (Page 13)

Peacock Music Studio Logo, DogStar Design, (Page 47)

table of*CONTENTS*

introDUCTION

by supon phornirunlit

The willingness, if not eagerness, to be entertained is a universal human trait. One obvious measure of the entertainment industry's importance is its size. Radio and television, movies, music, and theater are bigger today than ever. The last time we checked, Steven Spielberg's movie *Jurassic Park* had grossed over $300 million. Janet Jackson's album *janet* had sold over five million copies. Regional theaters and opera companies were alive and kicking almost everywhere. As you would expect, these separate industries combine to issue a profuse stream of images—images that seep into the most remote corners of the globe. One can find a poster advertising a distant Mozart performance in a tiny European mountain chapel, or an image of singer Michael Jackson painted on the side of a Tanzanian village restaurant. And this mélange of images designed to promote events, concerts, films, and other products requires a high level of both creativity and insight.

"Show business" demands powerful, often emotion-packed graphics to match the flash and intensity of the product. The box office success of many films has been enhanced by posters advertising them in advance. In this merchandising method, posters titillate the audience while withholding the actual product. Film promotions must captivate and even, to a degree, mystify audiences—and also, more and more often, initiate extensive marketing campaigns.

But entertainment graphics are just as often subtle and intensely personal. They can put the intrigue in the first release of an independent filmmaker, the emotion in a list of never-before-heard song titles, the electricity in the dark air before the curtain rises on the stage. Design for live theater or book jackets may be classically understated or joltingly experimental.

On T-shirts, posters, playbills, album covers, and elsewhere, graphics propel the excitement of show business. Commercial art can single-handedly draw audiences to an entertainment. Designers in the contemporary music field concur that an awareness of youth interests is critical for attracting audiences to bands targeting younger markets. But an appealing facelift on a classical recording cover can introduce even a baroque piece of music to new, appreciative audiences. As Laurence J. Peter said, "An ounce of image is worth a pound of performance." Design is what can create the image even before the performance is seen.

Just as the annual report and corporate stationery require their own set of approaches, a talk radio program or an avant-garde theater piece uncover their own special challenges. Performing arts, though charged with emotion and personality, can be difficult to define, and even harder to visualize. As Miles Davis once said, "I'll play it first, and tell you what it is later." But when the designer's vision is on-target, few other industries recognize and treasure outstanding graphic design as enthusiastically. The praise for the creative from the creative is a truly worthy compliment.

Designers enjoy working in entertainment for many reasons—most of all, perhaps, the variety of projects that come their way. They can create a realistic stagebill cover for a wrenching drama, and go on to produce impressionistic packaging for a set of commemorative cassettes for an operatic tenor, capturing his character in line and color.

For this book, we've chosen almost 300 of the finest graphics the entertainment industry has offered to date, from a wide variety of projects executed in various styles. They include everything from music store logos to packaging for films on videotape to posters for live theatrical events. We admire these pieces for their insight, originality, depth, and charm.

The entertainment industry gives designers great opportunity for discovering new forms of expression. Whether or not your client list includes well-known names, the pieces featured here will offer you new insights into commercial art. We hope you will be inspired, delighted—and, especially, entertained.

Supon Phornirunlit is principal of Supon Design Group, where he also serves as creative director. Since founding the studio in 1988, he and his design team have earned more than 600 industry awards, including recognition from every major national design competition. Supon has served on the boards of directors of the Art Director's Club of Metropolitan Washington and the Broadcast Designers' Association, and is a frequent speaker at various industry organizations and universities. The studio's work has been featured in such recognized publications as Graphis, Communication Arts, Print, Step-by-Step, Studio, *and* How Magazine.

3

commen *TARY*

by margo chase / margo chase design

IT'S A GLAMOUROUS LIFE

Entertainment design seems glamorous. People imagine that you spend your time at catered lunch meetings, gossiping with Madonna. The reality is often far from glamorous.

Music designers are able to do innovative work because the design approval process is limited to one or two people rather than large committees. While some record companies have in-house art departments with many designers and art directors on staff, the musician and one staff designer typically make the design decisions, giving designers room to express the music and themselves. This intimate process can have its drawbacks as well. When the musician is adamant about using some awful painting done by his girlfriend on the cover, there's little a designer can do but groan.

A memorable CD package might inspire a few design junkies to take a risk on something they've never heard, but for the most part, if someone likes the music, they'll buy the CD whether they like the cover or not. This explains why the design budgets for most releases remain small.

Music sales are dependent on radio air play and music videos, so getting the music played on the radio is crucial. This means getting the attention of radio D.J.s and station managers. Because the CD package format is small and all CDs come in the same boring plastic box, it can be difficult to make a particular group stand out. In an attempt to attract attention to new artists or projects, special promotional packaging has evolved. These are elaborately designed, limited edition packages which are sent out to radio station managers and record store buyers. For designers, these projects are a chance to break out of the plastic square and go wild. So much more money and ingenuity goes into the creation of these special packages that the Grammys have had to start a separate category for them.

In the music business, the constant push to stay current can be exhausting, but it also encourages experimentation. Computer graphics technology was quickly embraced by the record business as a way to ease the strain of impossible deadlines and budgets. Programs like Adobe Photoshop have taken costly retouching and image editing out of the lab and into the studio. Layout programs like QuarkXpress have made the process of typesetting and mechanical production seamless. Copy and lyrics from the record company come to the designer on disk. Completed digital mechanicals are sent back to the record company and then go straight to film. While working on a computer has its frustrations, the Macintosh has put more control into the hands of the designer and the results are both weird and wonderful.

Movie campaigns are believed to have a huge impact on the public's perception of a movie and, therefore, on its sales. This brings much more pressure to bear on the designer. For major movies, a studio will typically have several design firms working on the same campaign. The budgets for these presentations are often generous, but the time pressure can be insane. Each firm is expected to present 20 one-sheet ideas in as little as a few days. This gives the designer no time to refine a concept or layout. When you consider that the studio executives who make the design decisions are more concerned with a movie's profitability than the

aesthetics of its campaign, and that an adventurous design is perceived as risky and unsound, you can begin to understand why most movie campaigns look depressingly similar.

To make matters worse, the final approval for any one campaign may rest with committees of businessmen and lawyers who are using the results of market testing, previous movie experience, and the limitations of restrictive contractual agreements to make decisions. Internecine struggles between agents and studio lawyers result in contracts that define design details such as the relative sizes of names in billing blocks or the relationship between the size of art titles and the sizes of various stars' heads. The effect of all of this on the designer is lobotomizing. It's impossible to create a breakthrough poster campaign when one is forced to use five heads of specific sizes on one poster.

To avoid these restrictions, many design firms concentrate their creative energies on the design of teaser posters. These are preliminary posters in a campaign, not limited by the same strict contracts. Movies such as *Batman*

and *Hook* featured teaser posters that were far more compelling than their final one-sheet, because the designers could focus on one iconic image or series of images, rather than being forced to cram everything into a single poster.

While the movie business is a struggle for designers who value self-expression, the process can still be rewarding. Lucrative budgets permit experimentation and the use of technology not available to many. Movie designers were using high-end paint box retouching and image editing long before the Macintosh made computer graphics widely accessible. The budgets and the time pressures also encourage collaboration with other artists, photographers, and designers. Some beautiful work may never see the light of day, but creating it can keep designers going.

Whatever the reality of designing for entertainment, no one has to know you didn't lunch with Madonna.

5

commen *TARY*

by robynne raye / modern dog

THINGS WE WANTED TO DESIGN AND WHO WE WANTED TO WORK FOR

It was tempting to make up a bunch of high-minded, important-sounding reasons why we went to work in the field of entertainment graphics, but the plain truth is that we just wanted to do posters. As kids, we liked posters and album covers because the artwork on them was cool, and so different from anything else that was presented to us as "art." We all had collections of our favorite pieces and proudly decorated our suburban bedrooms with them. Mike's favorite album cover was Led Zeppelin's *Physical Graffiti*, probably because he's really a Peeping Tom at heart. Later, when we moved to Seattle and started Modern Dog, we were really impressed by all the posters hanging around town—particularly those of Dale Yarger and Art Chantry. Those posters—and the incredible proliferation of them—helped us in our decision to go after theaters as clients. We never thought of ourselves as entering the field of "entertainment graphics," and

we never had a climactic moment pointing us in that direction. Posters seemed like they would be the most fun out of all the kinds of work we felt were accessible to us as a new design firm. We were lucky to secure several theaters as clients right off the bat, and we can truthfully say that theater posters were our bread and butter for many years.

We've probably done more theater posters than any other kind of work, and we've realized a few things that make us like doing them even more. Posters are great because they aren't part of something else. They aren't packaging on top of some product, or a picture introducing a reader to a whole book full of words. Since posters aren't physically connected to what they advertise, they can take on an identity of their own. Precisely because of that, posters are one of the few forms of graphic design that can outlive their original function. In short, we believe that posters document culture. Sounds pretentious, but it's true. The posters that get collected are the ones that represent a certain time or feeling for the person looking at them. And when that happens, posters cross the line from advertising art to a diary of our culture.

But while posters are great, they don't exactly pave the streets with gold. By Modern Dog's second year of business, we had enough theater work to keep us pretty busy, but let's face it, we were starving. We didn't want to do annual reports or corporate brochures, but we sure did want to make rent. So we sat down one afternoon and made lists of what kinds of things we wanted to design and who we wanted to work for. The first list was full of stuff like record covers, candy wrappers, cereal boxes, pinball machines...fun stuff that we'd grown up admiring. The second list—the companies that we wanted to work for—included entertainment conglomerates like MTV, Warner Bros., and Capitol Records, as well as Nike and General Foods. A wide variety of companies selling a wide range of products, but with one thing in common: all of them seemed to have an appreciation for good, fun design (not to mention the budgets to back it up). So we went to work trying to get jobs from those com-

panies. We didn't spend any time developing a marketing plan or figuring out a five-year strategy. We just promoted the hell out of ourselves and stayed in contact with the decision-makers at each company. That's not to say we were irritatingly persistent. We wanted to make our interest and availability known, not bombard anyone with letters or phone calls. But we did send post-cards and self-promo goodies, and if we came up with a cool idea for a particular company, we sent it along. After a while, we got to know what people responded to and liked, and they felt comfortable giving us work.

And that brings up the whole subject of self-promotion. Whether the industry targeted is entertainment or manufacturing, self-promotion is about the most important thing a studio can do. We're not talking about a friendly card at Christmas time that says we've donated money to a favorite charity in your name (although that is a very nice thing to do), we're talking about finding the qualities that make us different from any other studio and publicizing them like crazy. We've always felt that our

name and crude (yet friendly) sense of humor were our most unusual attributes, and our self-promotion reflects that. We've come up with some pretty weird pieces, and some people haven't liked them. That's fine with us, because even though someone may not love our fur box, it certainly stands out. The pieces that are borderline obnoxious are the ones that are remembered most. And if it gets us a job we want or makes some-one laugh, it's worth the risk. We see too many pieces of self-promotion that are about as risky as a pancake. I mean really, who's going to hire you if your stuff looks like everyone else's, and you didn't even include candy?

air*WAVES*

absolutely

Radio and television have the ability to focus
tightly on world events and on your five-
square-mile township. With the advent of
cable, generations are growing up with a buffet
selection of entertainment, from situation comedies
to operettas, and with instant infomation.
Telephones make many programs interactive.
Some of the most interesting designs relating to
these media are included here, from annual
reports for networks to promotional pieces for
programs to videos.

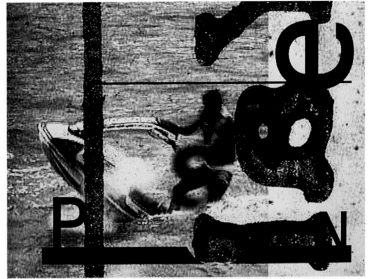

Title ESPN Video Promos
Design Firm Kampah Visions
Art Directors Flavio Kampah,
   Phil Delbourgo
Designer Flavio Kampah
Client Big Fat TV

10

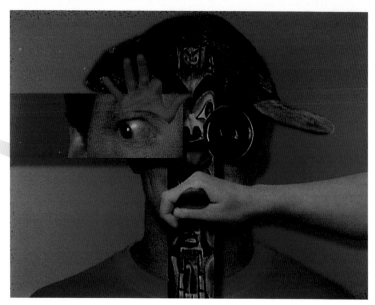

absolutely

Title "Royal Canadian Air Farce" Video
Design Firm Canadian Broadcasting
      Corporation
Art Director Tony Cleave
Designer Tony Cleave
Client Royal Canadian Air Farce

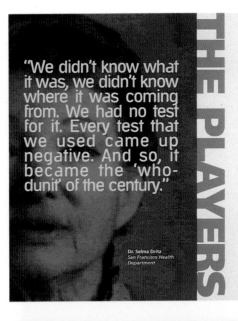

"We didn't know what it was, we didn't know where it was coming from. We had no test for it. Every test that we used came up negative. And so, it became the 'who-dunit' of the century."

Dr. Selma Dritz
San Francisco Health
Department

THE PLAYERS

A Time of AIDS features interviews with a wide range of key people who have been on the front lines fighting the epidemic, including:

Dr. Robert Gallo, the former head of AIDS research at the National Institutes of Health who became involved in a highly controversial race with the French to identify the AIDS virus;

Dr. Luc Montagnier, head of the Pasteur Institute's AIDS research team, who pioneered the French effort to find the AIDS virus;

Dr. Don Francis, the government scientist with the Centers for Disease Control whose job it was to work out how to control the spread of AIDS, and **Dr. James Curran,** former director of AIDS research at the CDC;

Roger McFarlane and **Larry Kramer,** founders of the Gay Men's Health Crisis and two of the first gay activists to mobilize the gay community against AIDS;

Dr. Selma Dritz of the San Francisco Health Department, one of the first people to recognize the onslaught of what would become known as AIDS;

Surgeon General C. Everett Koop, the top health official in the Reagan Administration;

Dr. Anthony Fauci, who oversaw the government's testing of experimental AIDS drugs.

The series also interviews the people most directly affected – AIDS victims, their families and loved ones – to provide a very personal view of the emotional effects of the disease.

The highly-charged real-life drama behind the AIDS epidemic is revealed as never before. The tragic stories behind the headlines come to life, including the hunt for the AIDS virus that turned prominent American and French researchers into intense and controversial rivals; the fatal decision by blood banks not to screen donors for infected blood until months after a test became available; the beginnings of the gay activist movement as a reaction to government inertia and cultural stereotyping; the black-market use of experimental AIDS drugs and the dispute surrounding the marketing of the ultimately unsuccessful "wonder drug" AZT.

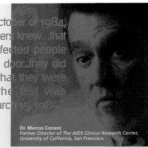

"As early as October of 1984, the blood bankers knew...that there were infected people walking in the door...they did not change what they were doing until the test was licensed on March 15, 1985."

Dr. Marcus Conant
Former Director of The AIDS Clinical Research Center,
University of California, San Francisco.

THE CONTROVERSIES

It was clearly seen as a gay disease, as self-inflicted...and there were tremendous problems getting people to accept that these people should be treated like any other patients... medicine maybe 600 years ago.

Dr. Michael Adler
Head of Venereal Disease Section
Middlesex Hospital, Great Britain

A TIME OF **AIDS**

DISCOVERY JOURNAL FOUR-PART MINI-SERIES,

TELLS THE REAL STORY BEHIND THE

EPIDEMIC THAT CHANGED THE WORLD.

JOURNAL Discovery

Title "A Time of AIDS" Press Kit
Design Firm Discovery Design Group, Discovery Communications, Inc.
Art Director Larnie Higgins
Designer Larnie Higgins, Richard Lee Heffner
Client The Discovery Design Channel, Discovery Communications, Inc.

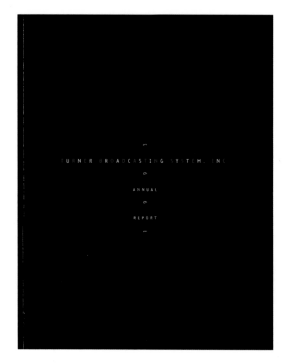

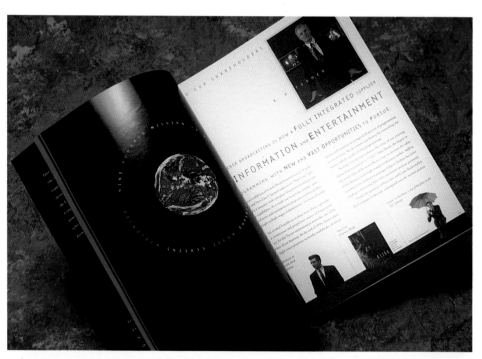

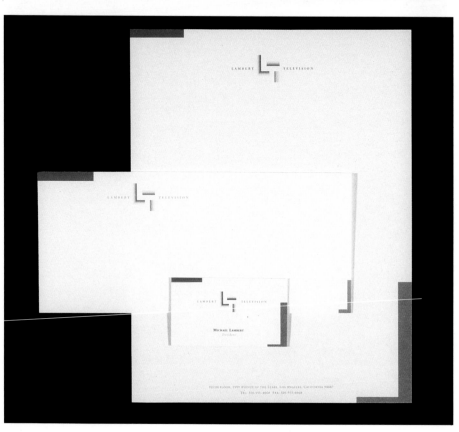

*ab**so**lutely*

Top

Title   1993 Turner Broadcast System, Inc.
              Report
Design Firm   Corporate Reports
Art Director   Brant Day
Designer   Kitsie Riggall
Client   Turner Broadcasting

Bottom

Title   Lambert Television Logo and
              Stationery
Design Firm   White & Associates
Art Director   Trina Nuovo
Designer   Byron Lee
Client   Lambert Television

USA CARTOON EXPRESS

On weekday and Sunday mornings and early fringe, you'll find kids across the nation catching the USA Cartoon Express, their TV ticket to today's animated favorites. From GI Joe to Teenage Mutant Ninja Turtles, USA's got the classic characters and contemporary cartoons that young people want most. For 26 1/2 hours each week, cartoon blocks on USA feature hot titles like Scooby Doo, Terrytoons, Chipmunks Go to the Movies, Ghostbusters, and Super Mario Bros. 3. They all add up to the most-watched daily cartoon block on cable!

ORIGINAL PROGRAMMING

USA Cartoon Express is speeding into the future with investment in new original kids' programming:

ITSY BITSY SPIDER

A tiny four-eyed, six-legged spider who avenges insect injustice, Itsy overcomes odds to save the day — whether he's liberating kids from a maniacal karate instructor or wreaking havoc on a TV cooking show! Itsy Bitsy Spider features the voices of The Facts of Life's Charlotte Rae and Max Headroom's Matt Frewer. It's a USA exclusive!

PROBLEM CHILD

In a world full of grown-ups, mind-boggling mischief rules, as Junior torments the neighborhood doctor's office, locks himself in the bathroom and gets a Presidential appointment! Seen exclusively on USA, Problem Child is based on the hit Hollywood comedy film of the same name.

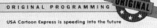 **USA NETWORK Kids**

from coast to coast

are holding on tight for the ride

of their lives with USA Network. For

rollicking, riveting, riotous cartoons on

USA Cartoon Express, the most

popular place on cable for today's

high-energy cartoons. For exciting chances

to win with The USA Network Kids Club.

Want details? Buckle up, 'cause it's

gonna be a wild ride!

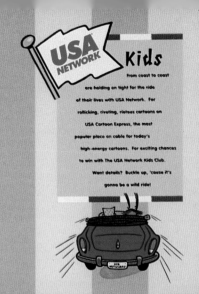

IT'S A WILD RIDE...

KID-TESTED TV FAVORITES: DRIVING THE SUCCESS OF CHILDREN'S PROGRAMMING

SCI-FI CARTOON QUEST

On weekday and Saturday mornings, kids beam up Sci-Fi Cartoon Quest, the only block on cable devoted to science fiction animation. Kids leap into the future with a brave new world of sci-fi cartoons like Terrahawks, Star Wars Droids: The Adventures of R2-D2 and C-3PO, Ewoks, Transformers, The New Adventures of Gigantor, Land of the Lost, Little Shop, Laser Patrol, Galaxy High School, Fantastic Voyage, and the animated version of Star Trek (featuring the voices of the original series cast). It's six days a week of far-out fun!

COSMIC CREW

Here's an added value opportunity for the next millennium. Cosmic Crew, a promotional tool with astronomical potential! Like USA Network's highly successful Kids Club, the Sci-Fi Channel's interactive Cosmic Crew vignettes give kids fun chances to play for prizes. Each Cosmic Crew vignette is specifically customized and exclusively produced to fit advertisers' special needs. Lift off with Cosmic Crew to reach today's young sci-fi fans; it's a unique new vehicle to showcase products!

SCI-FI CHANNEL KIDS PROGRAMMING SCHEDULE

Monday - Friday	
6AM-9AM ET*	SCI-FI CARTOON QUEST
Saturday	
7AM-11AM ET*	SCI-FI CARTOON QUEST

Title Kid's Presentation Brochure
Design Firm Laurie Kellihar/World Egg
Art Director Elisa Feinman
Designer Laurie Kellihar
Client USA Networks

absolutely

Title "Duckman Mailer" Promotion
Design Firm Diagraphics
Art Director Elisa Feinman
Designer Diagraphics
Client USA Networks

Top
Title   PBS Radio – FM Promotion
Design Firm   Value Added Design Pty
Art Director   Heather Towns
Designer   Heather Towns
Client   PBS Radio – FM

Bottom
Title   FOX Broadcasting '93-'94
               New Season Brochure
Design Firm   CBO
Art Director   John O'Brien
Designer   John O'Brien
Client   FOX Broadcasting

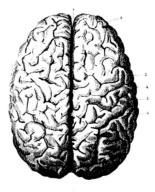

This Is Your Brain.

This Is Your Brain On BEAKMAN.

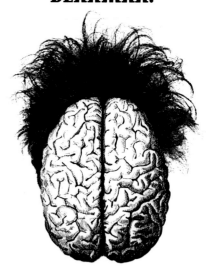

Everything you ever wanted to know but didn't know whom to ask.

Left

Title   Sci-Fi Satellite Gear Promotion

Design Firm   Peter Millen Design

Art Director   Elisa Feinman

Designer   Peter Millen

Client   USA Networks

Right

Title   "Beakman's World" –
          Brain on Beakman Ad

Design Firm   Columbia Pictures
          Television Distribution

Art Director   Ellen Stefani

Designer   Ron Taft

Client   Beakman's World

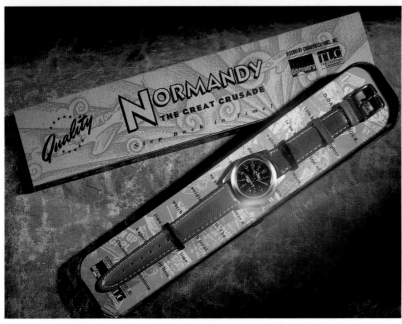

Title "Normandy: The Great Crusade"
　　　　Premiums
Design Firm Discovery Design Group,
　　　　Discovery Communications, Inc.
Art Director Richard Lee Heffner
Designer Richard Lee Heffner
Client The Discovery Channel, Discovery
　　　　Communications, Inc.

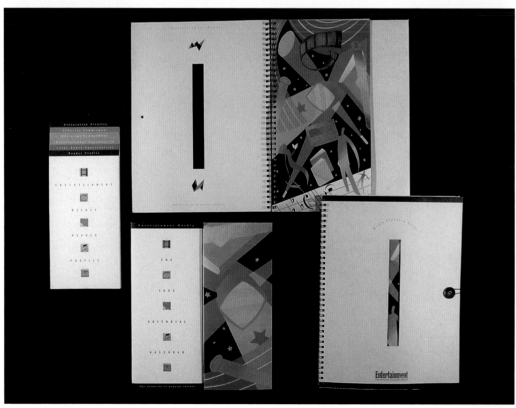

Top
Title   Upfront Ad Sales Materials
Design Firm   Discovery Design Group
              Discovery Communications, Inc.
Art Director   Larnie Higgins
Designers   Richard Lee Heffner,
              Mark Scheider
Client   Discovery Communications, Inc.

Bottom
Title   Media Kit for Entertainment Weekly
Design Firm   Platinum Design, Inc.
Art Director   S. Quinn
Designer   S. Quinn
Client   Entertainment Weekly

19

Title "30 Fragments 60 Fields" Promotion
Design Firm Kampah Visions
Art Director Flavio Kampah
Designer Flavio Kampah
Client Radius

Title BET Affiliate Sales Promotion

Design Firm Supon Design Group, Inc.

Creative Director Scott Perkins

Art Directors Supon Phornirunlit,
Andrew Dolan

Designer Andrew Berman

Project Directors LaTanya Butler,
Angela Scott, Matilda Ivey

Client Black Entertainment Television

Title Western Channel Promotion
Design Firm Colorado Production Group
Art Director Jeanne Kopeck
Designer Jeanne Kopeck
Editor Colin Spencer
Music Daniel Clason
Client Encore

22

absolutely

Title "Inside Washington" Program Open
Design Firm W*USA-TV Design
       Department
Art Director Mary Ruesen Strauss
Designers Mary Ruesen Strauss,
       Donna Beard
Animators Donna Beard, Scott Suess
Client W*USA-TV

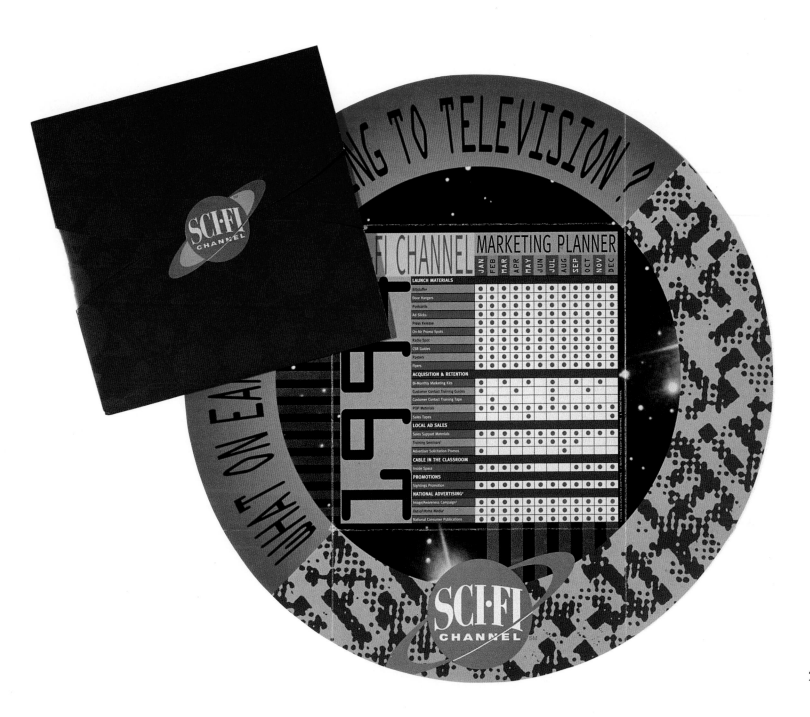

Title Sci-Fi Western Show Brochure
Design Firm Peter Millen Design
Art Director Elisa Feinman
Designer Peter Millen
Client USA Networks

24

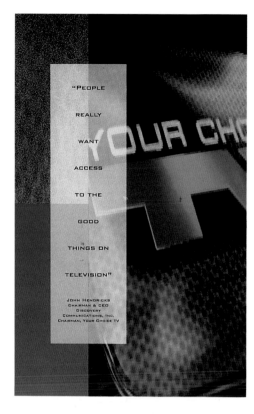

"PEOPLE

REALLY

WANT

ACCESS

TO THE

GOOD

THINGS ON

TELEVISION"

JOHN HENDRICKS
CHAIRMAN & CEO
DISCOVERY
COMMUNICATIONS, INC.
CHAIRMAN, YOUR CHOICE TV

Title Your Choice TV Letterhead and Brochure
Design Firm Supon Design Group, Inc.
Creative Director Gil Cowley
Art Directors Supon Phornirunlit,
    Andrew Dolan
Designers Apisak Saibua, Richard Boynton
Project Director Kathleen Hayes
Client Your Choice TV

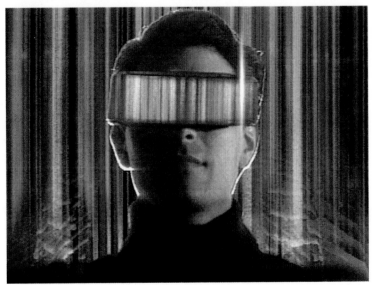

Title "Virtual Reality" TV News Promotion
Design Firm W*USA-TV Design Department
Art Director Mary Ruesen Strauss
Designer Mary Ruesen Strauss
Animator Karen Swenholt
Producer Mag Cumbow
Client W*USA-TV

26

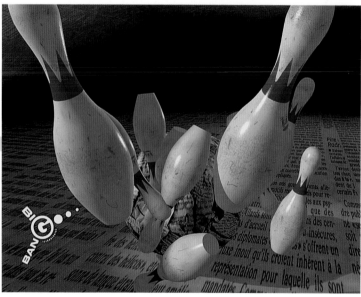

absolutely

Title "La Presse Sort II" Commercial Video
Design Firm Big Bang Technologies, Inc.
Art Directors Pierre Drovin,
        BCP Agency
Producer Danny Bergeron
Director Danny Bergeron
Production Big Bang Technologies
Client BCP Montreal

Title   BET on Jazz Brochure
Design Firm   Supon Design Group, Inc.
Creative Director   Scott Perkins
Art Directors   Supon Phornirunlit,
      Andrew Dolan
Designer   Anthony Fletcher
Photo Research   PhotoAssist, Inc.
Project Directors   LaTanya Butler,
Client   Black Entertainment Television

30

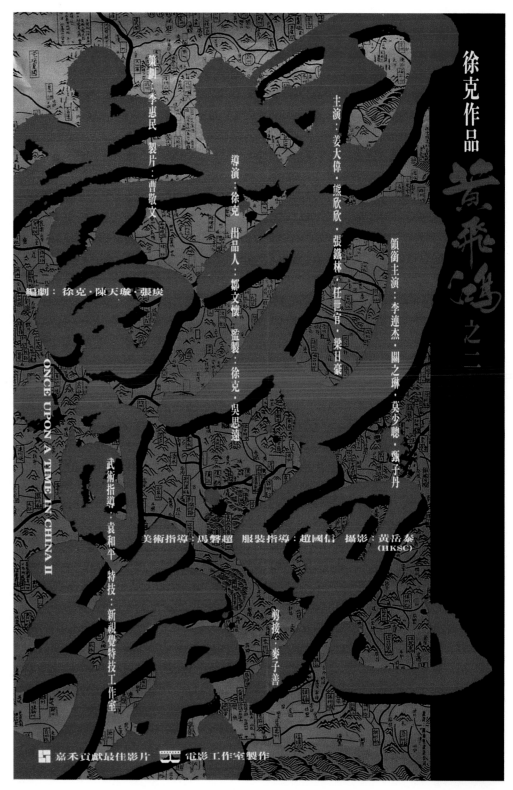

Title Once Upon a Time in China II
Poster
Design Firm Alan Chan Design
Company
Art Director Alan Chan
Designers Alan Chan, Peter Lo
Client Film Workshop, Ltd.

LONG LIVE THE EARTH

AND ALL HER SPECIAL GIFTS!

Left
Title Earth Vision Film Festival
Promotion
Design Firm Douglas Design
Art Director Douglas Doolittle
Designer Douglas Doolittle
Client Urban Communications

Right
Title Film Collections Logo
Design Firm Sabin Design
Art Director Alison Hill
Designer Tracy Sabin
Client Turner Entertainment Co.

32   **Title**   "Heaven and Earth" Promotional Film Identity
         Design Firm   Tim Girvin Design, Inc.
         Art Director   Tim Girvin
         Designer   Tim Girvin
         Client   Seiniger Advertising

Title   Rim Films Logo
Design Firm   PPA Design Limited
Art Director   Byron Jacobs
Designer   Byron Jacobs
Photographer   Ted Chin
Client   Golden Harvest

Title   Jeanne Evans/Actress Logo
Design Firm   John Evans Design
Art Director   John Evans
Designer   John Evans
Client   Jeanne Evans

Left

Title "Boat People" Film Poster

Design Firm PPA Design Limited

Art Director Byron Jacobs

Designers Byron Jacobs, Michelle Shek

Client Golden Harvest

Right

Title "Top Squad" Film Poster

Design Firm PPA Design Limited

Art Director Byron Jacobs

Designers Byron Jacobs, Michelle Shek

Client Golden Harvest

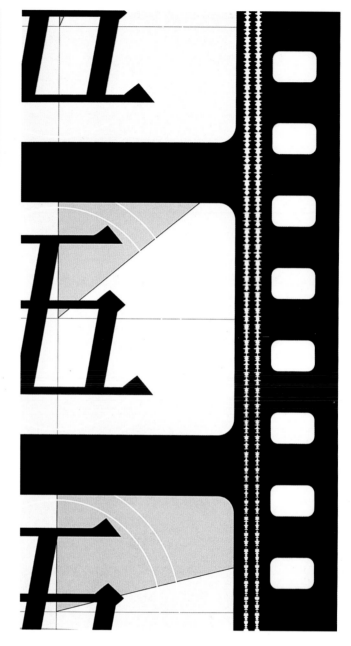

Golden Harvest
congratulates
The Fifth
Tokyo International
Film Festival

Golden Harvest

Left
Title "King of Chess" Promotion
Design Firm Alan Chan Design Company
Art Director Alan Chan
Designers Alan Chan, Alvin Chan, Chen Shun Tsoi
Client Film Workshop Co., Ltd.

Right
Title Fifth Tokyo International Film Festival Advertisement
Design Firm PPA Design Limited
Art Director Byron Jacobs
Designer Michelle Shek
Client Golden Harvest

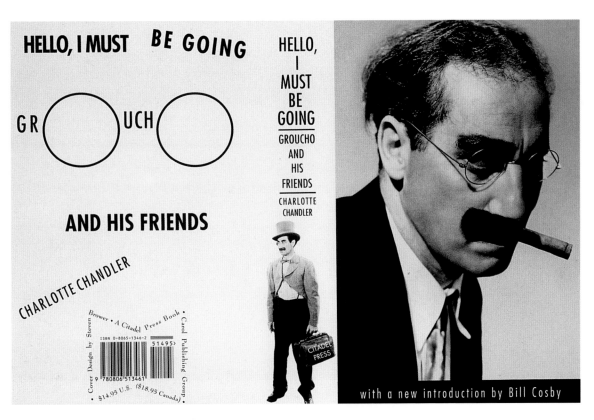

36

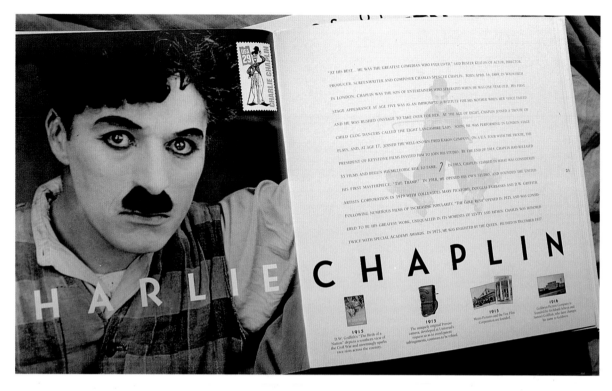

absolutely

Title "Legends of the Silent Screen" Book
Design Firm Supon Design Group, Inc.
Creative Director Terry McCaffrey
Art Directors Supon Phornirunlit, Andrew Dolan
Designers Apisak Saibua, Andrew Berman,
Dianne Cook, Richard Boynton
Editor Linda Klinger
Photo Research PhotoAssist, Inc.
Client U. S. Postal Service

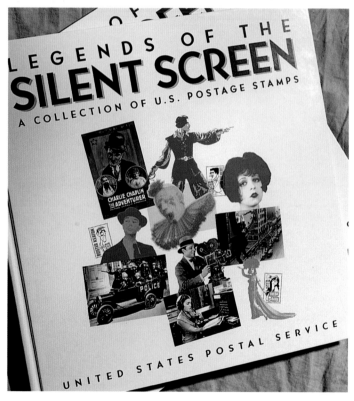

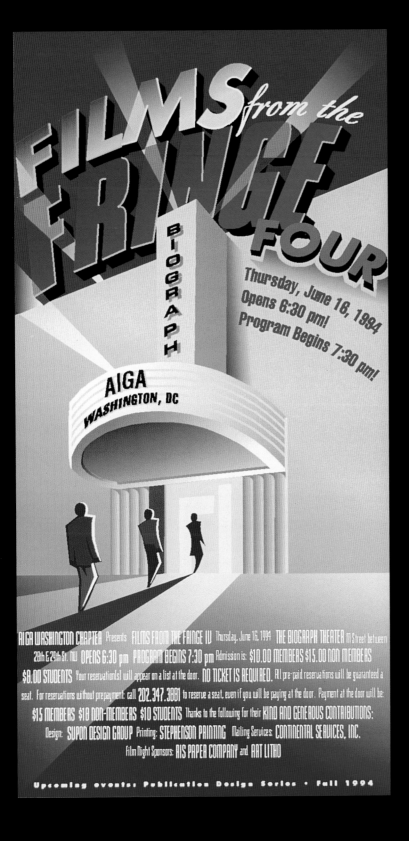

37

Title Films from the Fringe Poster
Design Firm Supon Design Group, Inc.
Art Directors Supon Phornirunlit, Andrew Dolan
Designer Andrew Dolan
Project Director Terry McCaffrey
Client American Institute of Graphic Arts

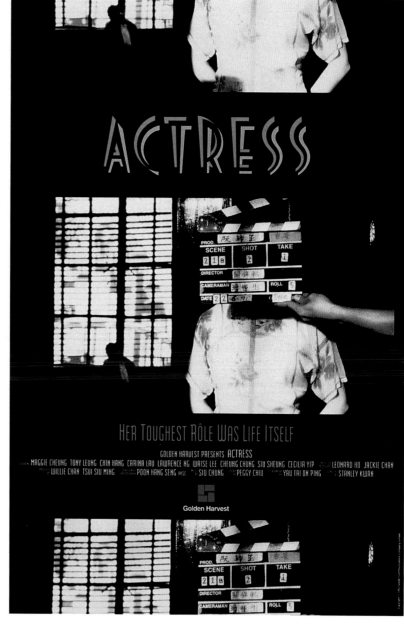

absolutely

Left

Title "Sex and Zen" Film Poster

Design Firm PPA Design Limited

Art Director Byron Jacobs

Designer Byron Jacobs

Client Golden Harvest

Right

Title "Actress" Poster

Design Firm PPA Design Limited

Art Director Byron Jacobs

Designers Byron Jacobs, Tracy Hoi

Client Golden Harvest

Title   Golden Harvest 1992 New Year's Card
Design Firm   PPA Design Limited
Art Director   Byron Jacobs
Designers   Byron Jacobs, Tracy Hoi
Client   Golden Harvest

40

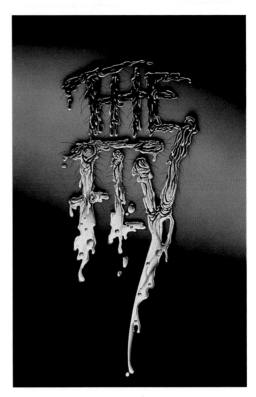

absolutely

Top
Title "Blown Away" Book
Design Firm Mike Salisbury
       Communications
Art Director Mike Salisbury
Designers Mike Salisbury, Patrick O'Neal
Client MGM

Bottom
Title "The Fly" Logo
Design Firm Mike Salisbury
       Communications, Inc.
Art Director Mike Salisbury
Designer Mike Salisbury
Client 20th Century Fox

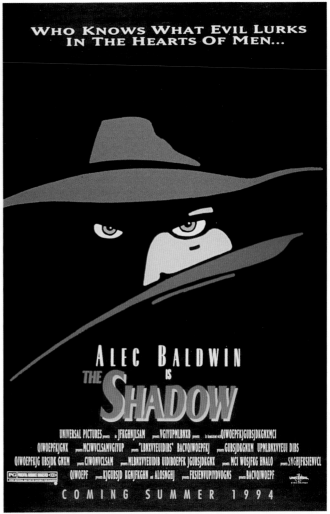

Left
Title "Younger & Younger" Poster
Design Firm Wueschner, Rohwer
Art Director Petra Barchfeld
Designer Andreas Rintzner
Client Jugendfilm/Berlin

Right
Title "The Shadow" Poster
Design Firm Mike Salisbury Communications
Art Director Mike Salisbury
Designer Mike Salisbury
Client Universal

42

FILM

absolutely

Top
Title Illinois Film Office Location Guide
Design Firm Kym Abrams Design, Inc.
Design Firm for Film Logo Zechman Associates
Art Director Kym Abrams
Designer Mike Stees
Designer for Film Logo Dick Lemon
Client Illinois Film Office

Bottom
Title "Meteor Man" Logo
Design Firm Mike Salisbury Communications
Art Director Mike Salisbury
Designer Mike Salisbury
Client MGM

Title "To Live and Die in L.A." Poster
Design Firm Mike Salisbury Communications
Art Director Mike Salisbury
Designer Mike Salisbury
Client MGM

tune*FUL*

absolutely

Music's roots reach back to the first human beings beating rhythms on a hollowed-out tree. Like the Olympic Games or a kiss, it does not need translation to be enjoyed. Various ways have been discovered to combine sounds, notes and tones into something lyrical, stimulating, haunting, and powerful. Music has incorporated words, bells, whistles, cannons, and computers. Here, we bring you some of the most successful designs influenced by this experimentation with sound.

45

Title Jazz Festival Willisau '93 Poster
Design Firm Niklaus Troxler
Art Director and Designer
    Niklaus Troxler
Client Jazz in Willisau

Title "The Four Chinese Beauties"
CD Packaging
Design Firm Alan Chan Design
Company
Art Director Alan Chan
Designers Alan Chan, Alvin Chan,
Cetric Leung
Client James Wong Productions Ltd.

POLYDOR

Title Polydor Logo
Design Firm Jay Vigon Studio
Art Director Jay Vigon
Designer Jay Vigon
Client Polydor

Title Peacock Music Studio Logo
Design Firm DogStar Design
Art Director Rodney Davidson
Designer Rodney Davidson
Illustrator Rodney Davidson
Client Peacock Music Studio

Title Gregory Freeze, Singer/Pianist Logo
Design Firm DogStar Design
Art Director Rodney Davidson
Designer Rodney Davidson
Illustrator Rodney Davidson
Client Gregory Freeze

absolutely

Top
Title Joice Walton CD Packaging
Design Firm Tollner Design Group
Art Director Jeff Dentino
Designer Christopher Canote
Printer A's Printing
Client Pinnacle Records

Bottom
Title South by Southwest Music Convention Ad
Design Firm Modern Dog
Art Director Laurie Burke
Designer Michael Strassburger
Copywriter Michael Strassburger
Client Warner Bros. Records

THE INDIANS
indianism

Title The Indians/Indianism CD Packaging
Design Firm PolyGram Records
Art Director Sheryl Lutz-Brown
Designer Sheryl Lutz-Brown
Client PolyGram Records

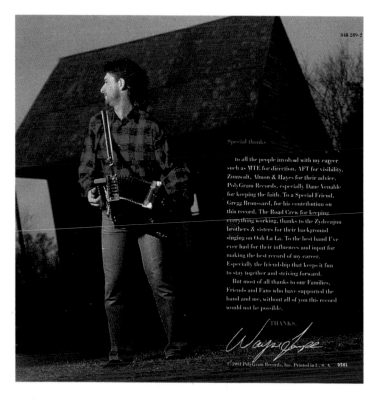

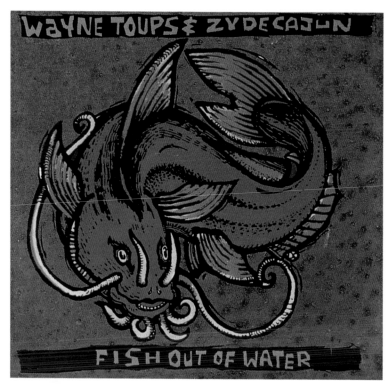

Top

Title Wayne Toups & Zydecajun/Fish Out of
Water CD Packaging

Design Firm PolyGram Records

Art Director Michael Bays

Designer Michael A. Klotz

Illustrator Donald Klotz, Jr.

Client Wayne Toups

Bottom

Title Yoko Owada "Evening of Mozart" Poster

Design Firm Hiromura Design Office

Art Director Massaki Hiromura

Designers Massaki Hiromura,
Takafumi Kusagaya

Client Million Concert Company, Ltd.

Top
Title Shou Dú CD Packaging
Design Firm Alan Chan Design Company
Art Director Alan Chan
Designers Alan Chan, Peter Lo
Client Music Factory

Bottom
Title Shou Dú Poster
Design Firm Alan Chan Design Company
Art Director Alan Chan
Designers Alan Chan, Peter Lo
Client Music Factory

53

54

Title Royal Concertgebouw Orchestra Invitation
and Program
Design Firm Leslie Chan Design Co. Ltd.
Art Director Chan Wing Kei.Leslie
Designers Chan Wing Kei.Leslie,
Tong Song Wei
Client Ing Bank

Top
Title Meat Puppets/Backwater CD Packaging
Design Firm PolyGram Records
Art Director Michael A. Klotz
Designer Michael A. Klotz
Client Meat Puppets

Bottom
Title Natraj/"Meet Me Anywhere" CD Cover
Design Firm design M design W
Art Directors James Westhall,
        Maureen Maloney
Designers James Westhall, Maureen Maloney
Digital Imaging Paul Roseneck
Calligrapher Maureen Maloney
Client Dorian Group, Ltd.

55

UTAH SYMPHONY
FIFTIETH ANNIVERSARY
Joseph Silverstein
Music Director
May 8, 11 and 12, 1990

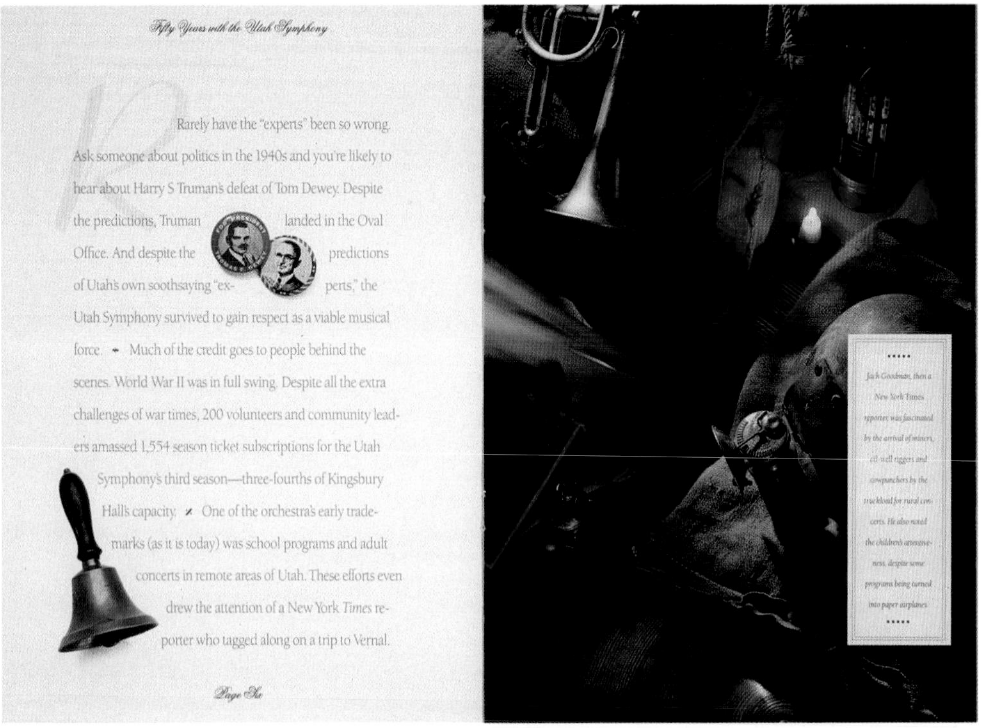
Fifty Years with the Utah Symphony
Rarely have the "experts" been so wrong. Ask someone about politics in the 1940s and you're likely to hear about Harry S Truman's defeat of Tom Dewey. Despite the predictions, Truman landed in the Oval Office. And despite the predictions of Utah's own soothsaying "experts," the Utah Symphony survived to gain respect as a viable musical force. Much of the credit goes to people behind the scenes. World War II was in full swing. Despite all the extra challenges of war times, 200 volunteers and community leaders amassed 1,554 season ticket subscriptions for the Utah Symphony's third season—three-fourths of Kingsbury Hall's capacity. One of the orchestra's early trademarks (as it is today) was school programs and adult concerts in remote areas of Utah. These efforts even drew the attention of a New York Times reporter who tagged along on a trip to Vernal.
Page Six
Jack Goodman, then a New York Times reporter, was fascinated by the arrival of miners, oil-well riggers and cowpunchers by the truckload for rural concerts. He also noted the children's attentiveness, despite some programs being turned into paper airplanes.

Our Roots are Showing.
Violent Femmes
Add It Up
The story of Violent Femmes as told by its participants. Featuring an all-new recording of "I Held Her In My Arms" PLUS a 22-track potpourri of unreleased demos, album tracks, answering machine messages, alternate takes, live performances, import-only b-sides and a radio spot. Whew. Reg.Price
Los Lobos
Just Another Band From East L.A.: A Collection
A double-album compilation featuring their best-known tunes, some practically unknown rarities and several impending hits. Including an all-new live version of the Marvin Gaye classic "What's Going On," "La Bamba" "Will The Wolf Survive?" and 38 more! 14.99 Cass 21.99 CD
BoDeans
Go Slow Down
These Wisconsin faves count among their influences everything from Eddie Cochran to Nelson Mandela, and the songs on their latest album are the most diverse and accessible ever to emerge from the songwriting partnership of Sam Llanas and Kurt Neumann. Including "Closer To Free" and "Feed The Fire." 7.99 Cass 11.99 CD
On Slash Cassettes and Compact Discs.
©1993 Slash Records.

absolutely

Top

Title Utah Symphony 50th Anniversary Program

Design Firm Richards & Swensen, Inc.

Art Director William Swensen

Designers William Swensen, Michael Richards

Photographer Dirk Douglass

Client Utah Symphony

Bottom

Title Our Roots Are Showing Billboard Ad

Design Firm Modern Dog

Art Director Kim Champagne

Designer Vittorio Costarella

Illustrator Vittorio Costarella

Client Warner Bros. Records

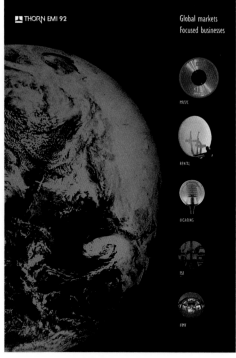

57

absolutely

Title   150 Proof Riddims CD Packaging
Design Firm   PolyGram Records
Art Director   Michael A. Klotz
Designer   Michael A. Klotz
Client   Mercury

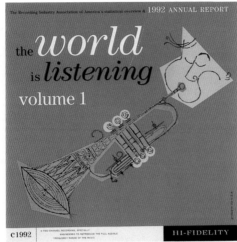

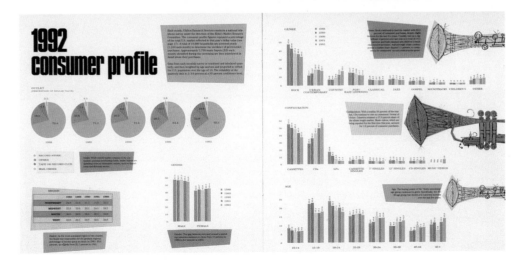

Title "The World is Listening" Annual Report
Design Firm Recording Industry Association of America
Art Director Neil Ashby
Designer Neil Ashby
Illustrator Dave Plunkert
Photographer Barb Kinney
Client Recording Industry Association of America

absolutely

Left

Title Together For the Cure Invitation

Design Firm Platinum Design, Inc.

Art Directors Sandra Quinn, Vickie Peslack

Designer Sandra Quinn

Client AMFAR Foundation

Right

Title "Working Without Annette" CD Packaging
and P.O.P. Display Unit

Design Firm Sayles Graphic Design

Art Director John Sayles

Designer John Sayles

Client The Flying Marsupials

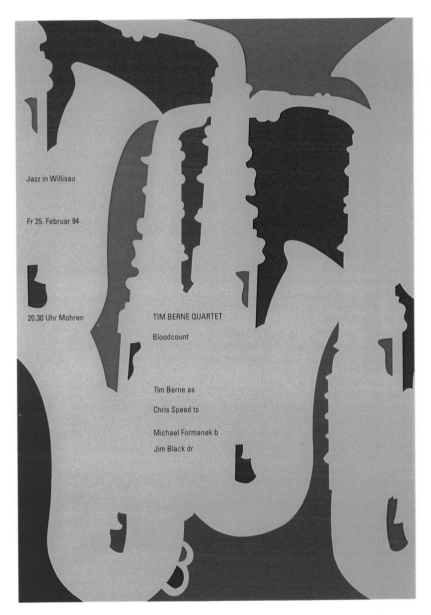

Jazz in Willisau

Fr 25. Februar 94

20.30 Uhr Mohren

TIM BERNE QUARTET

Bloodcount

Tim Berne as

Chris Speed ts

Michael Formanek b

Jim Black dr

Left
Title Jazz Festival Willisau '93 Poster
Design Firm Niklaus Troxler
Art Director Niklaus Troxler
Designer Niklaus Troxler
Client Jazz in Willisau

Right
Title Love + Rockets
Design Firm Modern Dog
Art Director Vittorio Castarella
Designer Vittorio Castarella
Illustrator Vittorio Castarella
Client Tasty Shows

Title "Even Better Than The Real Thing"
        Music Video
Design Firm Kampah Visions
Art Director Flavio Kampah
Designer Flavio Kampah
Client U2

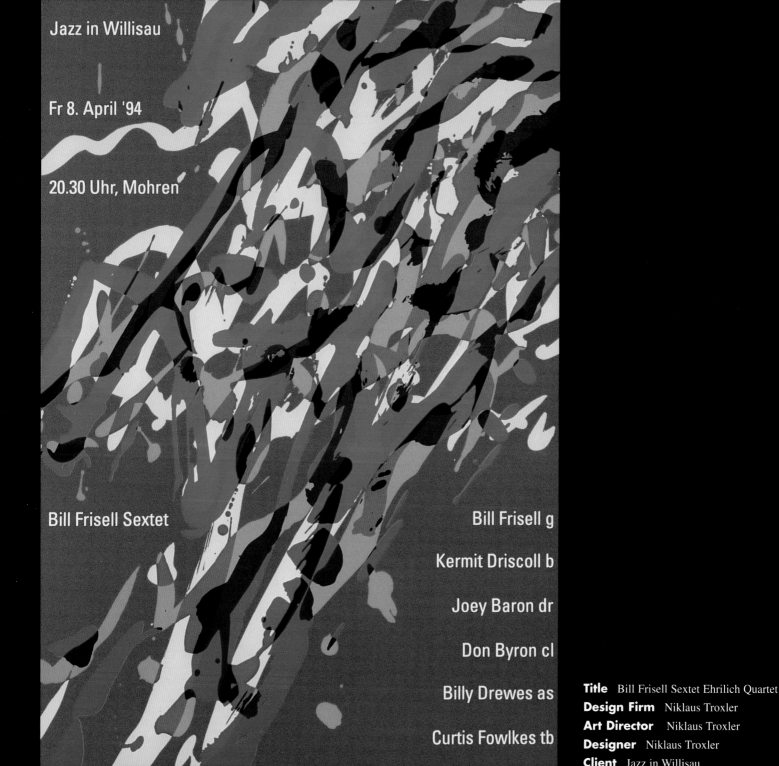

Jazz in Willisau

Fr 8. April '94

20.30 Uhr, Mohren

Bill Frisell Sextet

Bill Frisell g

Kermit Driscoll b

Joey Baron dr

Don Byron cl

Billy Drewes as

Curtis Fowlkes tb

Title Bill Frisell Sextet Ehrilich Quartet
Design Firm Niklaus Troxler
Art Director Niklaus Troxler
Designer Niklaus Troxler
Client Jazz in Willisau

absolutely

Title   Marty Ehrlich Quartet Poster
Design Firm   Niklaus Troxler
Art Director   Niklaus Troxler
Designer   Niklaus Troxler
Client   Jazz in Willisau

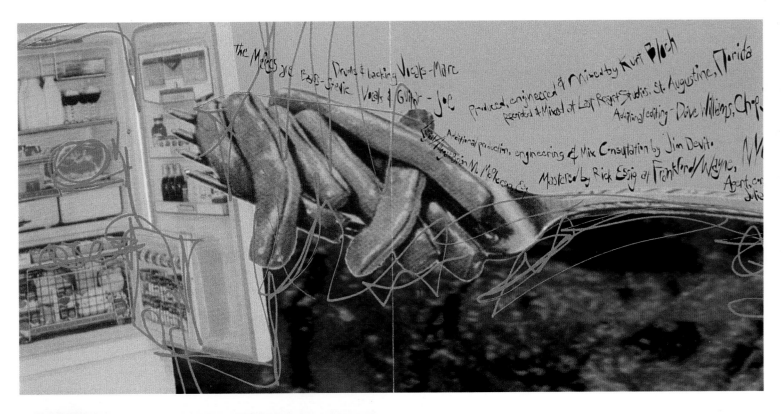

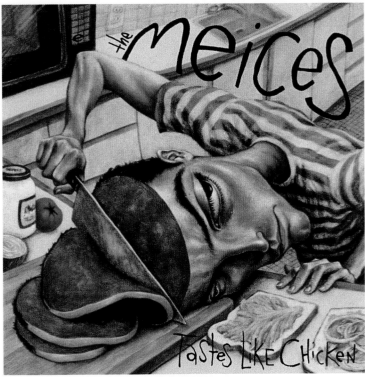

Title Meices/Tastes Like Chicken
CD Packaging
Design Firm PolyGram Records
Designer Patricia Lie
Illustrator Eric White
Client I.L.S. Records

absolutely

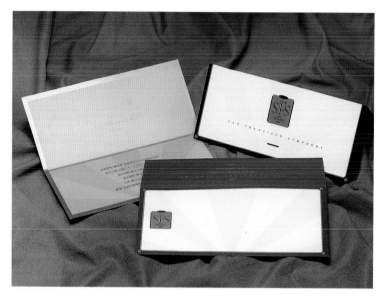

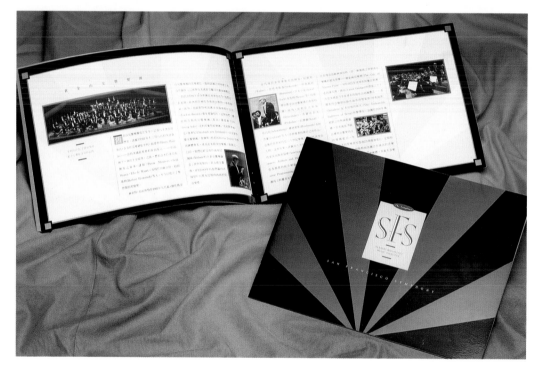

Title   San Francisco Symphony Identity
Design Firm   Leslie Chan Design Co. Ltd.
Art Director   Chan Wing Kei.Leslie
Designer   Chan Wing Kei.Leslie
Client   Amway Taiwan Limited

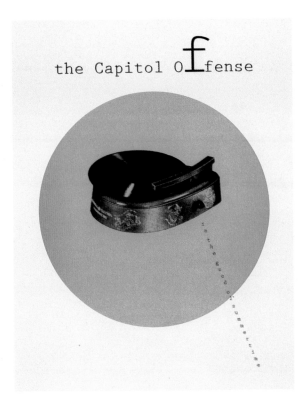

Title The Capitol Offense Magazine Covers
Design Firm Modern Dog
Art Directors for Big Orange and Free
Jeff Fey, Michael Strassburger
Art Directors for Trumpet Nose
Jeff Fey, Vittorio Costarella
Art Directors for Double Scoop
Jeff Fey, Robynne Raye
Designer for Big Orange and Free
Michael Strassburger
Designer for Trumpet Nose
Vittorio Costarella
Designer for Double Scoop
Robynne Raye
Client Capitol Records

70

Title Greta/Revolver CD Packaging
Design Firm PolyGram Records
Art Director Sheryl Lutz-Brown
Designer Sheryl Lutz-Brown
Client PolyGram Records

Title Seattle Camerata Logo
Design Firm Hornall Anderson Design Works
Art Director Jack Anderson
Designers Jack Anderson, David Bates
Photographer Seattle Camerata
Calligrapher Nancy Ogami
Client Dali Records

Title Kirk Alford/Piano Technician Logo
Design Firm DogStar Design
Art Director Rodney Davidson
Designer Rodney Davidson
Illustrator Rodney Davidson
Client Kirk Alford

71

Title Dewin Tibbs/Operatic Baritone Logo
Design Firm DogStar Design
Art Director Rodney Davidson
Designer Rodney Davidson
Illustrator Rodney Davidson
Client Dewin Tibbs

Top
Title   Sneak Peeks Logo
Design Firm   Rebecca Sobaje Design
Designer   Rebecca Sobaje
Client   JMC Acquisitions, Inc.

Bottom
Title   Logo for K. Lee Scott, Composer/Conductor
Design Firm   DogStar Design
Art Director   Rodney Davidson
Designer   Rodney Davidson
Illustrator   Rodney Davidson
Client   K. Lee Scott

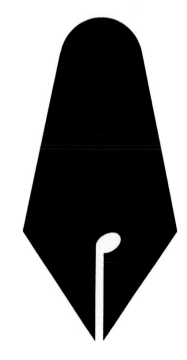

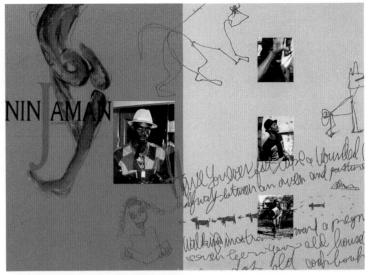

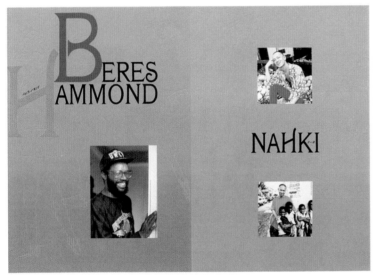

73

Title Reggae Japansplash Promotional Book
Design Firm Alfalfa Inc.
Art Director Takeo Aizawa
Designer Takeo Aizawa
Illustrator Shigeki Yamane
Client Tachyon Co., Ltd.

74

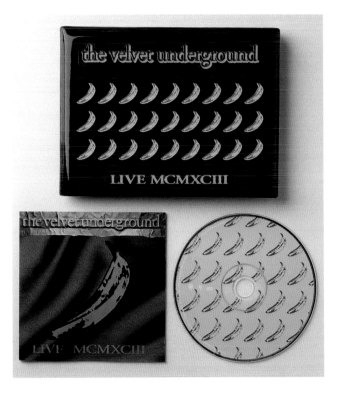

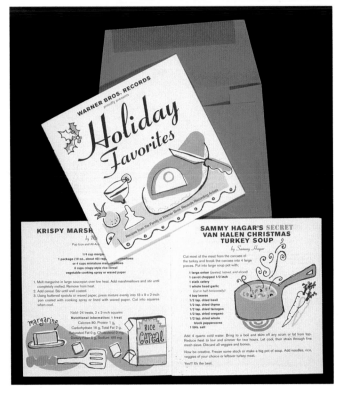

Top

Title Live MCMXCII/The Velvet Underground –
Retail Poster and Limited Edition CD Packaging

Design Firm Just Design

Art Directors Sylvia Reed, Spencer Drate, Jeff Gold

Designers Sylvia Reed, Spencer Drate,
Jütka Salavetz, Dennis Ascienzo

Photographer Ted Chin

Poster Production Chloe Harrison, Andrea Delregno

Client Sire/Warner Bros.

Bottom

Title Warner Bros. 1993 Holiday Greeting Cookbook

Design Firm Modern Dog

Art Director Jeri Heiden

Designers Robynne Raye, Michael Strassburger

Illustrator Robynne Raye

Client Warner Bros. Records

absolutely

Left

Title "Jazz Live at the Hyatt" Poster
Design Firm Sayles Graphic Design
Art Director John Sayles
Designer John Sayles
Illustrator John Sayles
Client Hyatt Newporter

Right

Title Wine & Food Showcase Poster
Design Firm Sayles Graphic Design
Art Director John Sayles
Designer John Sayles
Client Des Moines Metro Opera

absolutely

Left

Title "Flaming Lips" Poster

Design Firm Modern Dog

Art Director Vittorio Costarella

Designers Vittorio Costarella

Illustrator Vittorio Costarella

Client Moe Cafe

Right

Title "Better Than Ezra" Poster

Design Firm Modern Dog

Art Director Vittorio Costarella

Designer Vittorio Costarella

Illustrator Vittorio Costarella

Client Moe Cafe

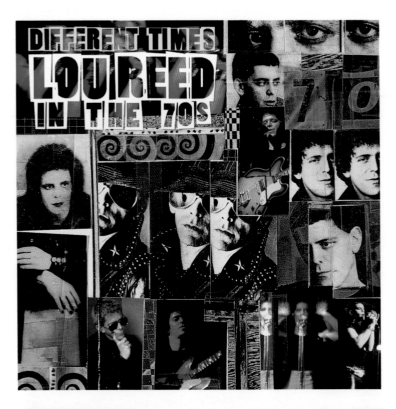

Top

Title Different Times, Lou Reed in the 70's
Design Firm Modern Dog
Art Director Naomi Taubleb, RCA Records
Designers Coby Schultz, George Estrada,
          Vittorio Costarella
Illustrator Coby Schultz
Photographer Daniel Arsenault
Client RCA Records

Bottom

Title The Kingston Trio, The Capitol Years
Design Firm Modern Dog
Art Directors Jeff Fey, Tommy Steele
Designers Vittorio Costarella,
          Michael Strassburger
Illustrator Vittorio Costarella
Client RCA Records

77

78

Title   Viva Italia!
Design Firm   Modern Dog
Art Director   Naomi Taubleb, RCA Records
Designer   Vittorio Costarella
Illustrator   Vittorio Costarella
Client   RCA Records

absolutely

Title Hello, My Name is...
CD Sampler for Music Convention
Design Firm Modern Dog
Art Director Jeri Heiden, A+M Records
Designer Michael Strassburger
Photoshop Michael Strassburger
Client A+M Recoeds

theat*RICAL*

absolutely

From school plays performed in gymnasiums to vast productions with full orchestras and famous stars, live performances reach all types of audiences. All you need to create theater is a performer and a spectator—add music and you have dance; add illusion and you have magic; add marionettes and children and you have Saturday morning at a museum. The posters, logos, and promotions included here are some of the best work highlighting the performing arts.

Title "One Mo' Time" Poster
Design Firm Bartels & Company, Inc.
Art Director David Bartels
Designer David Bartels
Illustrator Gary Kelley
Client Monsanto Foundation

82

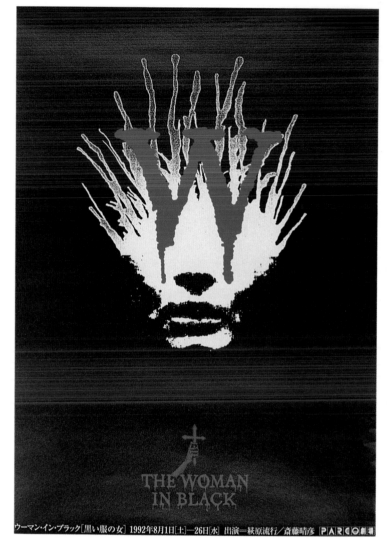

Title The Woman in Black Poster Series
Design Firm Hiromura Design Office
Art Director Massaki Hiromura
Designers Massaki Hiromura,
 Nobuhiko Aizawa
Client Parco Co., Ltd.

absolutely

このセリフが、まるで天から降って来たかの様に
私の頭に浮かび大いなる安らぎが私を包んだ。
私は、とり憑き離れない亡霊を断ち切る術は
被い清める事だと思いまして、そうだ。私も、被
い清めよう。あの話を語るのだ。私に書き記す
のだ、あらん限りの注意を払い、細大もらさず。
私独自の幽霊の話を書くのだ。それでみんなも
知り、私も永遠に破い清められ、語る事で記憶も
よみがえる。最初の作業書くことは終わった。
次は語ることだ。私は祈る、我々全てに、神の
御加護があります様に。

暗転。俳優、誕生。

THE WOMAN
IN BLACK

ウーマン・イン・ブラック［黒い服の女］1992年8月1日［土］—26日［水］ 出演─荻原流行／斎藤晴彦 PARCO劇場

84

absolutely

Title Coppélia Program
Design Firm Graphic Partners
Art Director Ron Burnett
Designer Andrea Welsh
Illustrator Emma Parker
Client The Scottish Ballet

Title Arlington's Arts al Fresco Logo Series
Design Firm Steven Morris Design
Art Director Steven M. Morris
Designer Steven M. Morris
Client Arlington County, Virginia Cultural
    Affairs Division

absolutely

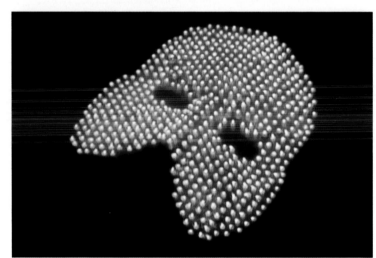

Title   "Candles" Video for "Phantom"
Design Firm   Echo Advertising & Marketing Inc.
Art Director   Jerry Huckins
Designer   Jerry Huckins
Copywriter for CD   Rob Simpson
Director   Dan Izzard
Client   Live Entertainment Corporation

Title Seasoned Performers Logo
Design Firm DogStar Design
Art Director Rodney Davidson
Designer Rodney Davidson
Illustrator Rodney Davidson
Client Seasoned Performers

Title Eugene Oniegan Logo
Design Firm Sabin Design
Art Director Kelly Davenport
Designer Tracy Sabin
Client San Diego Opera

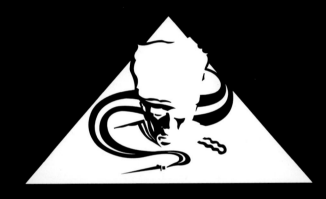

Title Arts Alive Logo
Design Firm Trudy Cole-Zielanski Design
Art Director Trudy Cole-Zielanski
Designer Trudy Cole-Zielanski
Client Frostburg State University

88

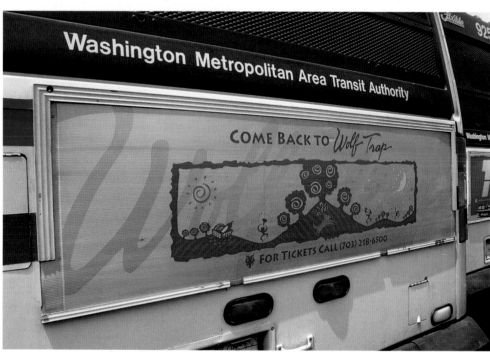

absolutely

Title Wolf Trap Promotion
Design Firm Supon Design Group, Inc.
Art Directors Supon Phornirunlit,
      Andrew Dolan, Steven Morris
Designer Steven Morris
Client Wolf Trap Foundation for the
      Performing Arts

Top

Title "Giselle" Promotional Literature
Design Firm Graphic Partners
Art Director Ron Burnett
Designer Andrea Welsh
Illustrator S. Parker
Client The Scottish Ballet

Bottom

Title "Phantom" T-Shirt
Design Firm Gregory F. Scott
Art Director Gregory F. Scott
Designer Gregory F. Scott
Client Theater Under the Stars

89

absolutely

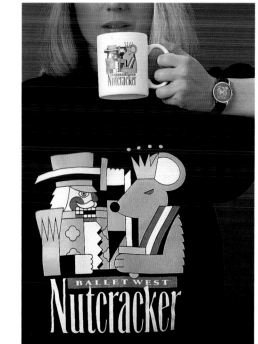

Title "Nutcracker" Campaign
Design Firm Richards & Swensen, Inc.
Art Director William Swensen
Designer William Swensen
Client Ballet West

91

Title Hats Off to Theatre X Poster
Design Firm McDill Design
Art Director Clayton Feller
Designer Michael Dillon
Copywriter Michael Dillon
Client Theatre X

Left

Title Theaterfieber Poster

Design Firm Niklaus Troxler

Art Director Niklaus Troxler

Designer Niklaus Troxler

Client Kleintheater Luzern

Right

Title Bil je skrjanec Poster

Design Firm KROG

Art Director Edi Berk

Designer Edi Berk

Client MGL (Town Theater of Ljubljana)

absolutely

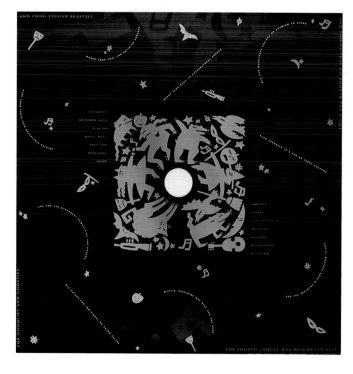

Left

Title Washington Software Association
Halloween Ball Poster

Design Firm Hornall Anderson Design Works

Art Director Jack Anderson

Designers Jack Anderson,
Julie Tanagi-Lock, Lian Ng

Client Washington Software Association

Right

Title "Kaj je Resnica" Poster

Design Firm KROG

Art Director Edi Berk

Designer Edi Berk

Client MGL (Town Theater of Ljubljana)

Top

Title Theatre X Hard Hats Brochure
Design Firm McDill Design
Art Director Clayton Feller
Designer Clayton Feller
Client Theatre X

Bottom

Title BRAVO BUS Logo
Design Firm DogStar Design
Creative Director Kevin Sutton
Art Director Jeff Martin
Designer Rodney Davidson
Client BRAVO BUS

miscel*LANEOUS*

absolutely

Anything that brings people together with the intention of amusing them, but doesn't fit into our previous four categories, is included here. Art festivals, craft fairs, carnival celebrations—even the occasional bird-calling contest—all fall under our general entertainment umbrella, along with pumpkin-hurling contests and hayrides. In most cases, the only thing these graphics have in common is that they are as entertaining as the events they promote or support.

101

Title 29th Bird-Calling Contest Poster
Design Firm Bartels & Company, Inc.
Art Director David Bartels
Designer Brian Barclay
Photographer Tom Ryan
Client Piedmont High School

Title Sunsplash '94 Poster
Design Firm Bartels & Company, Inc.
Art Director David Bartels
Designer Aaron Segall
Illustrator Gary Kelley
Client Earlham College

Title Full-Color Flyer
Design Firm Adriana Cortazzo
Art Director Adriana Cortazzo
Designer Adriana Cortazzo
Client Mister Good Bar

106

Left
Title   World Cup Pocket Guide
Design Firm   Supon Design Group, Inc.
Art Directors   Supon Phornirunlit,
            Andrew Dolan
Designer   Steven Morris
Client   ISM (Soccer) Inc.

Right
Title   Fremont Fair Poster
Design Firm   Modern Dog
Art Directors   Vittorio Costarella, Al Parisi
Designer   Vittorio Costarella
Client   Fremont Public Association

absolutely

Us convidem a la inauguració
del nostre bar Cue* Sant Cugat,
el dijous 30 de setembre de 1993,
a partir de les 20 h.
Us hi esperem!

Carrer St. Martí 12. (a 50m. C.A.P.-Creu Roja)
Sant Cugat del Vallès. Tel. 589 47 90

107

Title Cue Sant Cugat Invitation
Design Firm Sonsoles Llorens
Art Director Sonsoles Llorens
Designer Sonsoles Llorens
Client Cue Sant Cugat

Left

Title Artstorm Poster

Design Firm Hornall Anderson Design Works

Art Director Jack Anderson

Designers Jack Anderson, David Bates

Client Downtown Seattle Association

Right

Title Shiki Soku Ze Ku Poster

Design Firm Tad Co., Ltd.

Art Director Nobuyo Kataoka

Designer Nobuko Kataoka

Copywriter Kisoji Otori

Photographer Hideo Aomatsu

Client Osaka Design Center

109

Title Sandjam Posters
Design Firm Sayles Graphic Design
Art Director John Sayles
Designer John Sayles
Illustrator John Sayles
Client American Institute of Architects

110

*abso*lute*ly*

Title IBM's Olympic Sponsorship Identity
Design Firm Supon Design Group, Inc.
Creative Director Lee Green
Art Directors Supon Phornirunlit,
  Andrew Dolan
Designers Andrew Dolan, Andrew Berman
Illustrator Andrew Dolan
Client IBM

111

112

absolutely

Title Expand Your Horizon
Design Firm Sayles Graphic Design
Art Director John Sayles
Designers John Sayles
Illustrator John Sayles
Client Fort Dearborn

113

Title Iowa Department of Tourism Logos
Design Firm Sayles Graphic Design
Art Director John Sayles
Designers John Sayles
Illustrator John Sayles
Client Iowa Department of Tourism

114

Title   The Hit Parade and Ballyhoo,
The Sweet Cuisine of Broadway
Promotions
Design Firm   John Brady Design Consultants
Art Director   Mona McDonald
Designers   Rick Madison, Mark Murphy
Illustrator   David Bowers
Client   March of Dimes, Pittsburgh Chapter

absolutely